THE
HOSPITAL
OF THE
POOR

by

THOMAS À KEMPIS

Translated by Fr. Robert Nixon, OSB

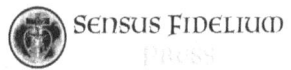

Sensus Fidelium
Press

Translated by Fr. Robert Nixon, OSB

ISBN: 978-1-962639-43-9

Book Cover, Interior, and E-book Design by
Amit Dey | amitdey2528@gmail.com

For more information, please visit sensusfideliumpress.com

TABLE OF CONTENTS

Translator's Note

Thomas à Kempis (1380-1471) is best-known as the author of *The Imitation of Christ*, a timeless classic which is regarded as being the second most popular and influential book on the Christian spiritual life after the Bible itself. Yet many people do not realize that he was an extremely prolific writer of other works as well, which run to several sizeable volumes in the original Latin.

This volume presents two of his shorter works which have not hitherto been available in English—*The Hospital of the Poor (Hospitale Pauperum)* and *The Way of the Monk: A Handbook for Spiritual Warfare* (*Enchiridion Monachorum*)[1]

Both of these treatises were written to serve as simple and helpful guides to the conduct of the spiritual life, and, because of this, are composed in a direct, straightforward and easily readable style. In this respect, many readers may find them a little more accessible than *The Imitation,* and a useful companion to that volume.

---

[1] Literally, *A Handbook of Monks.*

Thomas here gives very practical and concrete advice on how to grow in the Christian virtues, how to attain inner peace and contentment with one's situation in life, and how to fight effectively in the daily battle against vices. He writes not only as a great ecclesiastical scholar with profound knowledge of Scripture, theology and doctrine; but also as an experienced spiritual director and formator of novices, with marvelously penetrating and astute insights into the human condition.

It is the confident belief of the translator that this small volume will serve as a source of rich inspiration, encouragement and wisdom for all who read it. For the advice which Thomas offers us remains as relevant and practical today as it was in the 15th century, when it was written. No matter who we or what our situation is life, we are all, in some sense, poor; and we are all in need of hospitalization—not only to cure our inner failings and wounds, but to help us monitor and maintain our spiritual health for the future. Within these pages, you will find detailed remedies for vices, tepidity, bitterness and spiritual inertia; as well as useful prayers, practices and meditations to keep one's heart and life on the path which leads to eternal glories Heaven. May Christ keep us secure and faithful on that right path, until the day when we enter His Kingdom. Amen.

Fr. Robert Nixon, OSB
Abbey of the Most Holy Trinity,
New Norcia, Western Australia

THE
HOSPITAL
OF THE
POOR

i.

Detachment from All Worldly Honors and Riches

The Lord is my shepherd; there is nothing I shall want. Fresh and green are the pastures where He gives me repose.[2]

What could a person really gain for themselves from having all the riches and honors of this passing world? Ultimately, nothing more than enough food and clothing, which is all that a single individual can actually consume or make use of—and these simple things, in truth, can be obtained with far less effort and trouble. For human beings have limited genuine needs, consisting of sustenance and shelter, and anything which surpasses these is mere superfluity. Hence it is madness to be puffed up with pride or elation because one is rich or famous. And, what is more, these things disappear with the termination of this brief mortal life, and so have no more substance than

---

[2] Psalm 22:1.

the visions of a fleeting dream which vanished with the light of dawn.

Yes, when you leave this world, you will take nothing with you. You will have no more material possessions beyond the meagre cloth used to cover your deceased body, which will be consigned to the earth, just as, in a few short years, your name and memory will probably be consigned to oblivion.

But, O Reader, do not imagine for a moment that this means you shall not be held accountable for the use, good or bad, which you have made of this life. Indeed, God will call each person to deliver a full reckoning for whatever they have received, be it little or be it much. For these things are lent to us as provisions for this earthly pilgrimage of ours, but the Lord who has lent them will ask us what use we made of them, and enquire with exact reckoning concerning what profit we have gained for Him.

And so it is that the person upon whom more wealth, resources, talents and opportunities have been bestowed will not necessarily be accounted more holy or blessed than those who have received little or even nothing—unless, of course, they have obtained for the Lord correspondingly greater profits from the many things which have been entrusted to them. For the fact that a person possesses the passing and perishable treasures of this world does not imply that they will also be gifted with the true treasures which endure forever in the Kingdom of Heaven. Rather, the rich person is like a servant to whom much has been entrusted, and from whom much will therefore be demanded. God bestows riches on some for the purpose of bringing to fruition good and holy works; but how very often these same riches, which are a gift and responsibility from God, are abused as an opportunity to indulge more freely in sin and luxury!

Our merciful and just Lord will surely return to each one a fitting recompense; or, rather, such is His generosity and love that He will reward most magnificently those who are good servants, and in a way which far exceeds what they deserve. Thus for a little labor and effort, He will grant blissful rest which lasts forever; for enduring small and passing difficulties and tribulation, He will give unending, infinite joys; and for all the trivial humiliations and insults sustained during the course of this mortal life, He will bestow eternal glory.

In this present life, God gives to each person according to His own wisdom and good pleasure. God does this in a way which is determined by His own secret designs, plans and dispositions. These are utterly hidden and cannot be grasped or perceived by mortals; and yet we should not doubt that they are perfectly just and right, and without the slightest trace of error or miscalculation, in all times and places. For God orders all things for the good for those who are good, and similarly orders all things for the just retribution of those who persist in wickedness and sin.

No one should complain of the mysterious dispositions of Divine Providence, even though they may not understand them or fathom their purpose—for whoever does complain about the decisions and actions of God, which are infinitely beyond their comprehension, shows themselves to be ungrateful and unworthy. It behooves us to try to think well of our neighbor when we do not fully know the details of their actions and motivations, and to give them the benefit of the doubt; all the more, should we think only the very best of God, whose ways are as far above our ways as the Heavens are above the earth.

There was once a certain holy and honorable priest in Holland, who was preaching at the funeral of a nobleman, a Count of the Kingdom of Holland, who had recently passed away. He said to the people: "Our late master, a noble Count of this realm, has died. My beloved brothers and sisters, please pray for him. He was here on this earth for but a short span of life, during which time he possessed abundant wealth and income. But these he has now all lost, for he cannot take any of it with him where he has now gone. But the things which he *now* possesses, in the hereinafter, are not those dealt to him by fortune or inheritance of birth, but rather they are what he has deservedly gained through his own actions. The things which he owned on earth, he never truly possessed, but only held on a temporary loan; but what he has now is his for all eternity."

There is a story of another nobleman who had led a thoroughly wicked and depraved life, and was on the point of death. He spoke to his servants and friends who had gathered around him: "Alas for me! A simple shepherd who has taken good care of his few sheep is in a far better position than I am now, as I embark on that journey into the unknown from which there is no return!"

There was another very rich and illustrious nobleman, who was also drawing to the end of his earthly life. Now many people came to visit him, eager to secure a share in his legacy. Some of them were even so bold as to enquire of him: "My lord, what is it that you shall bequeath to me?" Upon hearing this, the ailing nobleman declared: "You are all interested in my wealth and property, but not one of you cares a jot for the fate of my immortal soul! And behold, I know not whether I shall still be alive to see the sun rise tomorrow morning." And thus he passed away, reflecting that all the earthly things in which he had placed his hopes had proved to be an empty deception, and had vanished from him like smoke which is blown away, or like mist which vanishes light of the sun.

Happy, rather, is the poor person who is rich in virtues! For such a person will be able to say with the Psalmist: "The Lord is my shepherd; for nothing shall I want. He makes me to rest in lush and verdant pastures, for His own name's sake."[3]

---

[3] Psalm 22:1-2.

ii.

The Five Breads of Spiritual Nourishment in the Desert of this Life

Man does not live by bread alone, but by every word which comes from the mouth of God.[4]

Our Lord God and our Savior spoke to the people of ancient times of yore through the Law and the Prophets. Today, He speaks to us each day through the Sacred Scriptures, both in the Old and New Testaments, and through all the holy and wise interpreters of these words over the centuries. For these words instruct us in what we should believe, in how we should live, and how we ought to serve God.

Therefore, I urge you to read and copy these words of Scripture with eagerness and diligence, as well as the commentaries of the saints upon them. For these ancient sacred texts have contributed to the salvation of a great many, and continue to do so to this present day.

---

[4] Matthew 4:4.

It is said that a certain holy priest once declared: "It makes no difference to me whether I happen to read the Old Testament or the New Testament, for I find the exact same saving message and truth in both. For it was the same God who inspired both!"

It is said that once, after the recitation of the Divine Office, Master Gerard, of the Brotherhood of the Common Life, asked one of the brethren: "Have you understood well what you have just read?" The brother replied: "Some of it I did understand. But, alas, not all!" The venerable teacher then told him secretly that each line of the psalms contained form him a multitude of mystical meanings, which had revealed to him over the years the infinite and varied graces of God.

O Reader, accept for yourself the five breads of spiritual nourishment which the Lord has provided for you! For these five breads of spiritual nourishment will help to sustain you as you make your way through the desert of this world, and they shall guide you securely to live in a virtuous and holy manner which is pleasing to God.

The first of these breads of spiritual nourishment is contrition of heart and sorrow concerning any past sins committed in your earlier life. The second bread is the act of making verbal confession for all sins and failings of the present time (and to recognize these as almost daily occurrences). This involves also identifying any sins of omission, such as any negligence in duties or prayer or indifference in the performance of good works. The third is the bread of divine consolation experienced through prayer, and the hope of God's mercy and His kind forgiveness of our sins.

The fourth bread of spiritual nourishment is giving thanks to God for all the benefits and blessings received from Him. This should be done both in times of prosperity and happiness, but equally in times of adversity and challenge. For all that He provides for us (whether it is pleasant or difficult), may God be blessed! For truly His mercy is without end or limit, and He has continually bestowed good things upon us in love and wisdom, from the beginning of creation right through until these present times.

The fifth bread of spiritual nourishment which sustains us on our pilgrimage through life is the grace of heavenly contemplation and internal spiritual jubilation. Such internal jubilation arises from the confident hope and anticipation of the eternal beatitude and glory which awaits us in our celestial homeland, which we shall one day share with God Himself and the whole communion of saints.

O Reader, give thanks to God for these five breads of spiritual nourishment which He provides for us, in order to sustain and strengthen as we make our arduous journey through the desert of this present world. And do not cease to praise and thank Him for the multitude of other gifts He has so generously given us—namely, all the benefits of nature and grace, and, above all, for the promise of eternal glory!

iii.

The Two-Fold Combat between
the Flesh and the Spirit

Lord, the wicked and ill-intentioned tell me many far-fetched and untrue stories, striving to distract me from fidelity to Your law. But I will guard all my senses, lest I am seduced by the vain and deceitful tricks of the devil and the world.

For as long as any human being lives, they must be engaged in battle of one kind or another. If they relax and let their guard down for even a moment, they shall be overcome by their temptations and vices and by the malicious attacks of the devil, who is the sworn enemy of every human soul.

But temptations do not always occur to us in the same manner, or with equal intensity. Nevertheless, it behooves us always to cry out to the Lord in Heaven with the same persistence and perseverance, with sincere prayers and heart-felt sighs of contrition.

What we call the "flesh" is whatever drags us downwards, while the spirit is that which leads us upwards. The flesh desires always whatever is pleasurable, soft and gratifying. The spirit, on the contrary, seeks that which is challenging, purifying and uplifting. If you choose to follow the promptings of the flesh, you shall inevitably be deceived and disappointed; but if you pursue the noble call of the spirit, you will achieve a crown of everlasting glory. For the flesh and the lusts thereof must inevitably perish, but the spirit is, by its very nature, immortal.

My Friend, attend to this combat diligently, and be vigilant on every front of this battle! For wherever and whoever you are and whatever situation in life you happen to occupy, you are always liable to the spears of your foe. These attacks are both external and internal, and both overt and covert; they assail us from the outside, but also spring up from within the depths of our own being.

A sure defense is to fix your heart firmly on the sacred wounds of Christ, our Savior. Let Jesus and Mary be your guardians throughout life, and you shall never be defeated. Take devotion to Christ and his glorious Mother to yourself as your trusted weapons; grasp them in your hands, like a flaming sword and an impenetrable shield!

Do not spend much time talking to the foolish, ignorant and vain. Neither should you cultivate conversation with the arrogant, opinionated and pretentious. For in spending your time speaking to persons of either type, you run the risk of slipping into sinful speech, or at least hearing words which will damage your spiritual life and focus. Rather, try to associate with people who sincerely love God, and who are humble, straightforward and faithful.

For cultivating good company and speaking of holy things helps the soul to love God and to seek after those things which are right and good. Conversely, bad company and gossiping about vain and worldly concerns confuses the conscience and inflicts untold damage upon the soul.

Above all, beware, O Reader, of the double-tongued and the two-faced! Rather, learn to enjoy the company of those who are of few words, and are quiet and straightforward.

iv.

The Instability and Inconstancy
of the Human Heart

My soul seems to be constantly disappointed and frustrated with my life! Why is this so, I wonder? The simple answer is that it is because of the many pains, stresses and toils to which I am subject; for all of these separate me from the eternal and perfect joy for which my heart truly longs. What, therefore, am I to do? To whom should I turn?

O my Soul, endure patiently and sustain these passing things with fortitude! Confidently place your hopes in the Lord, and wait for Him. For the Lord is always near to those who suffer tribulation in their hearts, and He will most certainly save those who trust in Him with a humble spirit.

For this reason, presumption and pride are to be studiously avoided, for these things alienate us from God, and lead us to resent the difficulties and sorrows of this present life. Rather, it behooves us to recognize that we suffer and are afflicted in this world quite deservedly and justly—for the sufferings of this world are all the product of sin, either our own personal vices and misplaced attachments, or the original sin which casts its shadow over all the poor, exiled progeny of Adam and Eve.

Whenever you hear yourself being criticized or sense yourself to be held in contempt or disdain by others, reflect for a moment on your own sins and vices. Then let your objections and complaints be silenced! For even if you are innocent of the faults of which you are now being accused, you know that you are certainly guilty of many other things which deserve similar treatment.

No-one (including both myself and yourself) is completely free from sin and stain; no-one is innocent. If we are honest, we must recognize that we have indeed all sinned very greatly, either in our actions or in the privacy of our own heart. It is God alone who is pure and innocent. It is God alone who is holy, eternal, immense and perfect. Therefore it makes sense for you to place all your hopes and trust in God, and to accept, with goodwill, whatever His mysterious plan assigns to you, whether it is prosperity or adversity.

For all the joys of this passing world quickly fade away and come to nothing. And all the praise and glory of this world is filled with deceit and falsehood. All the pleasures of the flesh have particular sufferings which inevitably accompany them. For example, gluttony and drunkenness lead to weakness and illness of the body; and lust leads to distraction of the mind and sorrow of the heart. And each sin brings disgrace and opprobrium if it is exposed to the world, and confusion and anxiety to the soul and conscience if it is concealed in secret.

In this world, the person who possesses much is burdened with great anxiety and responsibilities. But whoever is content with a little will be afflicted with fewer cares and stresses. Most truly miserable are the misers and the avaricious, who will never be content, no matter how much they own. But blessed is the one to whom God is all in all. Such a person will be able to say, along with the apostle St. Paul: "Let me not boast of anything, except in the cross of my Lord Jesus Christ, through whom the world has been crucified to me, and I to the world!"[5]

We read in the book of Proverbs about those who are lazy and half-hearted in the service of the Lord, where it is written: "The slothful both wills, and does *not* will it at the same time!"[6] The meaning of this is that such a person wills to eat and drink well, but does *not* wish to work or to fast. They wish to sleep for long hours, but do not wish to arise energetically and promptly. They desire to gossip and chatter, but do not desire to study and pray. They wish to correct others, but do not wish to be corrected themselves. They want to tell other people what they should do, but have no taste for improving themselves or reforming their

---

[5] Galatians 6:14.
[6] Proverbs 13:4.

own lives. People of this type are deserving of the rod and the lash, unless they amend themselves from all the faults described here, which, together, amount to grave hypocrisy.

But whoever remains constant and stable in the Christian virtues, or at least sincerely and consistently tries to cultivate them—such a person will be blessed forever and ever! Amen.

V.

The Obedience of the Simple and Humble Person

The person who is obedient may be accurately described as a conqueror and a victor. "Why is this?" the wise person will ask. It is because the person who is able to obey others with simplicity and humility has conquered his own ego, and is victor over his own selfishness. By being able to free himself from the constraints of his own preferences and bodily and mental impulses and submit himself to the commands and judgments of another, he has overcome the enemy who is most difficult to defeat—that is, self-will.

The person who has succeeded in doing this most heroic and noble thing will achieve for themselves great peace. For their conscience will be serene and untroubled, and consequently their heart will be filled with indescribable joy. Such persons will place their hopes in God and find their delight in Him alone. For this reason, they will be liberated from the fear of death itself, and no earthly suffering or hardship will be able to crush or depress them.

Good works which are performed in simple obedience to the divine will and commands are the most pleasing thing which can be offered to God. The one who obeys his legitimate superiors, and is ever willing to defer to his equals and even to give way to his inferiors—such a person confuses and frustrates the wicked devil, and so casts him down defeated. For it is the devil who implants the evil impulse to resist others, and who provokes resistance to simple obedience. For the enemy of our souls knows very well that such resistance gives rise to conflicts, argument, disharmony and many forms of evil, and destroys mutual love, fraternity and peace.

Our Lord Jesus taught us this lesson both by His words and His example. He calls us to simple obedience to God, and to the will of God as mediated through others. For He said: "Learn from me, for I am meek and humble of heart."[7]

The person who obeys another human being, solely for the sake of a higher obedience to the Lord and following the example and teachings of Christ, really gives the greatest possible honor to God, and becomes most pleasing to Him. Without the virtue of obedience, all of our good works possess little merit. On the other hand, an apparently trivial or insignificant work done out of pure and simple obedience, and out of charity and consideration of others,

---

[7] Matthew 11:29.

possesses the greatest merit in the sight of God—indeed, more so than an apparently heroic or arduous work performed out of pure self-will or personal preference.

True obedience is never hesitant, sluggish or slow to act. Neither is it negligent or half-hearted, and it is never accompanied by grumbling and resentment. The truly obedient person is ready to do absolutely anything which they know to be pleasing to God. A person may exercise obedience through the performance of any number of activities. They may pray or work, keep vigil or sleep, speak or keep silence. An obedient person may stand or walk, write or read, come or go, eat or fast. Each and every one of these activities, if performed out of obedience, becomes meritorious. This merit comes, not from the activity in itself, but the spirit of humble obedience with which it is performed.

The person who successfully conquers his own self-will becomes the genuine master of himself and of the whole world. He will enjoy peace and tranquility, and will be ever ready to obey the will of God, as expressed through the words of his legitimate superiors or the contingencies and duties of any particular situation.

> O holy angels of heaven, open to this blessed and virtuous person the gleaming gates of Heaven, and put to flight all the demons of pride which would seek to ensnare and deceive him!

> O Patriarchs and prophets, be his counsellors!

O Apostles and Evangelists, be his companions!

O all you saints of Christ, lend him your assistance to persevere in holy obedience!

When such an obedient person departs from this world and leaves behind the bonds of this mortal flesh, he shall surely rest happily in the bosom of Abraham, with the blessed poor man of the Gospel, Lazarus. And on the last day, he shall certainly enter into eternal glory with God and all of His saints. Amen.

vi.
The Triple Seal of the Holy Cross

"Place Me as a seal of divine love upon your heart, to love Me, the Lord, above all else.8 Inscribe the sign of My holy cross upon your chest. Let My sacred wounds be to you shields against all the spears and attacks of the enemy. For My Cross is the way of salvation, and the sigil of victory and triumph. It is an impenetrable shield which puts to flight all the perils of both body and soul!"

Thus speaks the good Jesus to each one of us. O Reader, it behooves you to place the seal of the holy cross upon three key places as a guard against all the vices: on your heart, on your mouth, and on your arms.

The seal of the cross, if inscribed upon your heart, will protect you from all evil thoughts. Rather, it will ensure that your thoughts are always of good things, and that you are ever mindful of the glory and beatitude of God and constantly thankful for His innumerable blessings. Guard your heart against all bitterness and malice, and do not let

---

8 Cf. Song of Songs 8:6.

them gain entrance! For wherever the sign of the cross is found such things are unwelcome. They retreat, for they find themselves out of place. For this powerful sign brings about a mystical and mysterious union with the love of God Himself, and with the virtues of all His saints.

Seal your mouth also with the sign of the cross, lest you speak of things which are evil, frivolous or presumptuous. Speak rather only of matters which are good, holy and edifying, for by doing this, you shall be acceptable and dear to God. And not only this, but your fellow human beings will come to respect you and be improved by hearing your conversation.

Place the sign of the cross also upon your arms, and upon your hands and fingers. For by doing this you will avoid wicked and godless acts, and instead work in a manner which is filled with true piety. And in everything you do, undertake to bless and praise God through all your actions.

In every place and time, strive to think only good thoughts, to say only good words, and to perform only good actions. Seal your heart, your mouth and your hands with the sign of the holy cross, so that your entire life may be brought into conformity with the saving passion of Christ. For through the cross, you will become capable of overcoming all temptations. The temptations which assault the human soul are many and varied—some come disguised as joy, while others come dressed in the garb of sorrow; some exhibit sweetness and delight, while others are flavored with bitterness. And all of these temptations can appear suddenly and unexpectedly, arising in the heart as if from nowhere and without any particular reason.

O Reader, there is barely anything you can undertake in this world, including even the most meritorious and holy works, which the devil will not attempt to subvert or hijack in some way. For Satan never ceases to attempt to draw us into evil, and to pollute and discolor our consciences with the stains of sin and vice. Do not even for a moment consider the things with which the devil tries to tempt you, but shun them all as if they were the foulest of dung!

Invoke the name and example of Jesus, and arm yourself with the weapon of the cross. Fly to Mary, our blessed Mother, as she stood so faithfully and unwavering by the cross of her divine Son, and stand there with her. Desire nothing else than to live always in the company of Jesus and Mary. For in doing this, you are guaranteed entrance into the eternal tabernacle of Heaven. Amen.

vii.
The Virtue of Merciful Compassion for the Sick

Support each other in charity, for charity cover up a multitude of sins.[9]

No-one should be focused entirely on themselves and their own well-being, and no-one should look upon the sick and suffering with disdain, contempt or indifference. For none of us know what lies in store for ourselves: tomorrow, it may very well be it is we who are sick and in need of the help and patience of others.

For we mortals are all fragile, and we all need help during our lives, at some times and in some ways. We all naturally desire what is good for ourselves, and are repelled by what is bad; and, just so, we should be concerned also to seek the good for our brothers and sisters, and minimize or alleviate whatever is bad for them. Therefore, my Friends,

---

[9] 1 Peter 4:8.

be merciful to each other, as the Lord teaches us, even as your heavenly Shepherd is merciful to you!

Do not be excessively rigorous, demanding or inflexible in your dealings with others, lest you become hard-hearted or insensitive to the weaknesses and infirmities which may afflict them. For if you are excessively rigorous and inflexible, you will only embarrass or hurt those who are not strong enough to conform to your expectations. Instead, you should aim at consoling and encouraging those who are struggling in any way. In this way, you will truly help them. Look upon others with mercy, rather than judgement, as much as possible.

The holy priest Florentius[10] used to declare: "I have converted many more souls by mercy than by strictness and terror!" This is something consistently proven to be true by experience, and it is this that Christ also teaches us. However you treat your neighbor in this life, whether it is with mercy or judgment, is how you will be treated when you yourself are judged. For Christ told us that "the judgments you give will be the judgments you receive."[11]

And whatever good act you do towards your neighbor who is suffering, sad or afflicted in any way, you do to Christ, and thus become like an angel ministering to the Lord

---

[10] Thomas is here referring to Fr. Florentius Radewyns (c.1350-1400), who was Master of the Brotherhood of the Common Life, a religious fraternity of which Thomas had been a member before becoming an Augustinian.

[11] Matthew 7:2.

God Himself. Therefore always be attentive and solicitous about the needs of others.

And ensure that you spend your time in a manner which is useful and gives praise to God. For everything which you have received and possessed is a gift from God, including life itself, and the capacity to understand, to think, to speak and to act. If you endeavor to give glory to God in the exercise of all of these gifts, you will certainly ascend to God with His angels. But when you seek empty vanity and earthly praise through these same gifts, or use them simply to please yourself, then you will surely fall down and be diverted from the prize of Heaven. You will lose grace, and gain in return only torment and trouble. It is the devil who has sown vanity and the desire for earthly praise into your soul—it is not, therefore, your fault if you happen to discover them lurking in your heart. But it *is* a sin if you do not immediately cast them away from you, and try your best to expel and uproot them.

For all those who are elated with pride and all those who glory in their own imagined merits render themselves foul in the sight of God and His holy angels. But the one who is humble and treats all others with goodwill and kindness, and shows mercy to the poor and compassion to the suffering, and offers comfort to the sorrowful and kindly instruction to those who err—such a person will enjoy the blessing and mercy of God during the course of this earthly exile, and in the world-to-come they shall inherit life everlasting. Amen.

viii.
Perseverance in Good Resolutions

Wait here, and stay awake with Me.[12]

Thus did Jesus urge His disciples to stay vigilant and to persevere with Him, even as He prepared Himself to undergo the ordeal of His passion, and to suffer the death whereby He would save us all.

Whoever wishes to dedicate their life to prayer and to being a true disciple of Christ[13] ought to bear these words always in their heart. They should imagine that Christ Himself is saying to them personally: "Wait here, and stay awake with Me. Pray earnestly, and prepare yourself for future trials and temptations. I Myself have given an example of keeping vigil and being steadfast in prayer, both for you and for others. Follow this example. Imitate Me, your Lord, and persevere in the good work you have commenced!"

---

[12] Matthew 26:38.
[13] In the original text, this reads "whoever has entered a monastery or a devout congregation." The adaptation presented above reflects the fact that the advice is applicable to Christians in all states of life.

Whoever holds steadfast until the end will be saved and will win the prize of victory. Those who are good will suffer many trials, tribulations and temptations; but they shall also receive many comforts and consolations along the way. And the sufferings of this present life cannot be compared with the glories which await in eternity for them.

Whenever temptations and tribulation arrive, let prayer also be immediately present. Do not despair or give up on your good intentions, but stand firm and commit yourself entirely to the God. Blessed indeed is the person whom suffering, affliction and temptation makes cautious, humble, merciful, gentle, compassionate, kindly, and contemptuous of no-one. And blessed is the community of faith where Jesus in their midst, and He Himself is their life, their virtue, their peace, and the harmony of their conduct.

But do not be shocked or scandalized, or agitated, or filled with fear, or depressed, if you should happen to witness some shortcoming or failure among your brothers and sisters in the faith. Do not be surprised or horrified is someone does not persevere in some good work they have begun, or if you encounter grumbling and complaints about hardships and deprivations (be they real or imagined), or if they lose enthusiasm for accustomed devotions or pious activities.

For we mortals are all weak and inconstant creatures. We are very much prone to failures and faults, but lethargic and unreliable when it comes to doing good! If it were not for the grace of God helping us, who is there who could persevere in a meritorious life, and resist the snares of the vices and temptations? Not myself—that is for certain!

But with God helping us and strengthening us, we are able to do all things. Not only can we begin with good intentions and holy resolutions, but we can persevere in them and bring them to happy fulfillment and completion.

But be cautious always in evaluating your own actions and discerning your own motives. For God finds fault even among His angels, and the first man, Adam, was expelled from the Garden of Paradise over so apparently small a matter as a mere apple! And many of the Israelites, as the wandered through the desert, came to perish, because of their disobedience, their murmuring against God, and their desires for fine and luxurious food. Indeed, even when Christ Himself was still present, defects and failings arose amongst the community of apostles—for some of them argued about who would be the greatest in the Kingdom of Heaven, and resentment and indignation arose in the hearts of the others. And Jesus reacted to this with a most merciful and mild correction, and He taught them by both His word and example to serve each other with humility, and to love each other with pure charity.

May the same Jesus Christ Our Lord help us all to do the same! Amen.

ix.

The Various Snares of our Ancient Enemy, the Devil

Stand up against the devil, and he will flee away from you![14]

"But how am I to do this?" you ask. Through faith, and through the power of the cross of Jesus Christ. "What shall my weapons be?" you enquire. My Friend, arm yourself with each of the following:

- vigils and fasts;
- toil in the day and prayer at night;
- sacred reading and devout meditation;
- poverty of spirit and chastity of the flesh and the heart;
- humility and simplicity; with silence and restraints from all vain conversations;

---

[14] James 4:7.

- solitude and withdrawal from the tumults of the world;
- compassion for the afflicted;
- supplication for your adversaries;
- perfect obedience and patience;
- strong and courageous battle waged against the vices;
- perseverance in the practice of the virtues;
- self-denial; and,
- disdain for worldly honor and human praise.

The one who sedulously takes up these strong weapons of the faith, as well as all other holy activities, and perseveres with them—such a one is pleasing to God, and is able to withstand all the attacks of the devil with unwavering fortitude!

For the wicked devils lays more snares for those who are religiously-minded than for anyone else. For he hates them more than he does others, because they are more focused on God than on the world. Consequently, he never ceases to tempt them, agitate them and try to scare them away from their commitments. But there is no-one at all who is ever free from the attacks of the devil or immune to the various snares which he lays so cunningly, regardless of their state of life, or age, or place of residence, and regardless of what religious order they may belong to.

What, therefore, are we to do? We are to fly to the Lord! We are to cry out to Jesus, with weeping and lamentation, imploring Him to help, strengthen and guard us! O Reader, pray to Him earnestly that after the many perils and tribulations of this present life, He may lead you to that wonderful place of true and eternal peace.

O, how blessed and wise is the person who renounces all the desires, pleasures and ambitions of this earth, and shuns from all the many and varied pathways of sin and iniquity! Blessed is the one who cultivates solitude and prefers to be unknown to others, and disentangles themselves, as far as possible, from the business of the world.

How useful and fruitfully does that person employ his time who contemplates daily the life and passion of Christ, and loves it in his heart, and seeks to imitate it in his conduct! Such a person will cast of all empty thoughts and vain curiosities, as well as all selfish ambitions and desires—in short, everything which distracts the mind and separates the heart from God. And very often they will think about their destined end, when they will arrive in the awesome presence of God, including the moment of death and the terrible judgments which awaits each one of us.

Faithful and prudent is that servant who follows the examples of the humility of Jesus, and spurns the broad and easy path which leads to perdition! For the devil lays his snares most profusely where riches, power and status abound, and it is principally through luxuries, delights and honors that he deceives and destroys his victims. Thus it is that those who live in simplicity, obscurity and poverty are safest from his nefarious clutches—but we should by no means image that even they are completely safe, either! For it often happens that those of poor and humble station look upon the rich and powerful, and their hearts are filled with a most covetous desire.

But Christ teaches us something quite opposite to this desire for the things of this world. For He said to the man who wished to acquire eternal life: "Sell all you possess, and give the money to the poor."15 For, indeed, the things which we imagine that we possess are not truly ours, for we did not create them, and neither shall we possess them permanently. Do not store up for yourselves treasures on this earth, for here all things are destined to perish very quickly. Rather, store up your treasures in heaven, where they shall last forever.

Flee from the concerns and allurements of this wicked world, and follow Christ! For in doing this, you shall certainly escape hell, and enter with Him into the eternal glories of Paradise.

---

15 Matthew 19:21.

x.

The Shield of Goodwill against Enemies

Let the Truth be the shield which protects you! For then "you shall not fear the terror of the night," as you pass long hours in nocturnal prayers and vigils; nor shall "the demon which prowls at noon" overcome you, as you are occupied in daily toils, good works and acts of self-denial.[16] Jesus Christ, as your way, your truth, your life, your salvation, your virtue and your wisdom, will be with you always. He will protect you both on the right and the left sides, in everything that you do—including all your works, and all your acts of worship and prayer. He will be your helper, your guard, and your strong protector against all the foes who assail you. And "if God is for us," as St. Paul says, "who can be against?"[17]

My Friend, do you wish to be free from all forms of fear? Then love Christ with all your heart! For the more the love of Christ increases in your heart, the weaker shall become

---

[16] Cf. Psalm 90:5.
[17] Romans 8:31.

your love of the things of this world. And where love of the things of this world has been extinguished, all fear and anxiety is likewise put to rest—for all earthly fear is ultimately the fear of the loss of earthly things, and where no attachment exists, then neither is there any possible cause for fear.

The person who is completely filled with love of God does not even fear death itself, or the devil, or hell. Grasp firmly, therefore, the shield of goodwill, in the love of God! For it shall dispel and destroy all fear, and expose all the frauds and deceptions of the devil.

Goodwill, by its very nature, is repelled by all evil, and, in turn, it is repugnant to evil and repulses it from itself. It avoids sin and all occasions of sin scrupulously; it rejects whatever is contrary to the truth and disproves what is false. It puts all deceptions to flight, and it detests all that is vain and wicked. Goodwill seeks to please God and is in itself pleasing to Him. It loves all that is good, true, just and holy, and wishes to honor the Lord in all things, both in actions and words, and in every place and time, as long as it abides in this world.

The person who is infused with goodwill will share the joy of every boon and blessing, regardless of to whom it falls and by whom it is experienced. It will be saddened by every misfortune and every sorrow, and will do its best to assist those who are in need, both friends and foes. It will be ready to forgive those who offend, to show compassion to the afflicted, and to offer gentle and humble guidance to those who err.

A good and perfect will causes a person to have God always before the eyes of their heart, and to be constantly mindful of His presence. It will sincerely love and esteem the virtues and merits of others, as pleasing to God, no less than if they were their own. It will be quick to give way on questions of personal will, preference and judgment. Furthermore, it will avoid attracting praise, and flee from popular fame and wide reputation. It will regard all things which separate it from God or do not honor God in some way as mere vanities and follies, and will be perfectly content with whatever suffices for the simple fulfilment of what is truly necessary.

O my Friend, if you find yourself afflicted with poverty or deprivation or affliction of any kind—do not be discouraged or overcome with pain and despair! For through your suffering, you participate in those of Christ on the cross, and you should not doubt the Christ also shares *your* sufferings. If your tribulations come as a result of following Christ, or even if you offer these sufferings up to God, you may count yourself to be a companion of the holy martyrs, who underwent agonies by fire, sword and beast, and in the dark confinement of ancient dungeons.

O Soldier of Christ, put up with the slight and short-lived afflictions which you now experience with patience and fortitude! Reflect for a moment on the countless saints who have tolerated much greater things, and all the while exhibited nothing but perfect tranquility and joy. You, who could not endure the torments of the saints and the harsh beating and tortures they sustained, should at least be able to put up with a few verbal insults, slights and offences!

Consider also what you sustain for your faith in Christ. Now, observe the kind of things which worldly people undergo quite willingly, merely to gain riches, success, power, or whatever it is to which they aspire—toil, late nights, sleeplessness, and peril; as well as (very often) insults, envy, defamations, and detractions from their rivals and fellow men. If they are prepared to endure such things for the sake of the passing prizes of this fallen world, how much more willingly should you be prepared to suffer and fight for the sake of a Kingdom which lasts forever, and a crown of glory which shall never fade nor be stolen away?

In all your tribulations and trials, call to mind the passion of Jesus Christ, and you will discover that your own sufferings immediately seem much lighter and more bearable. There is not one single person in this world who does not encounter their allotted share of pain and sorrow, both of the body and of the soul. There is no-one who escapes toil and pain under Heaven, for such is the common lot of mankind. Each one of us has our own burdens, heartbreaks, frustrations and disappointments. These come about either through oneself or through others; they arrive in the midst of activity and busyness, but likewise they are there in times of rest and apparent peace.

Our journey through this mortal life demands patience from us, and this is possible only through the grace of God. Take up the shield of a goodwill as your defense against the spears of the enemy, the vices of the flesh, and the deceptive allurements of this world. O you who would be the servant and soldier of God, clothe yourself with the armor of Christ; fight as a good and faithful soldier, adhering with loyalty to your Commander, the Crucified One!

The entire life of Christ was a cross. You should not expect anything different. For He Himself said: "Whoever wishes to come after Me, let him take up his cross daily, and thus follow me into My Kingdom."[18]

---

[18] Cf. Luke 9:23.

xi.
Praising God through Good Works

Praise the Lord, my Soul![19]

Every good work you do should be directed to the praise of God, and offered up as if it is an act of worship to Him. Whenever you have thought, spoken or performed any thing which is good, holy or meritorious, say in your heart at the end of it: "To God be praise: to God be thanks!" For without God and without His grace, human beings are able to achieve nothing which is truly good—they cannot begin it, and they cannot persevere well and virtuously, and they cannot bring it to a successful and happy conclusion. For God is the Alpha and Omega, the beginning and the end, of every good deed. It is God who grants the grace, the opportunity, the ability and the goodwill; so, in every good work offered to God, He receives only what He has first given and reaps only what He has first sown.

Cast from yourself, therefore, every tendency to pride, self-congratulation and vainglory! Rather, let your response be

---

[19] Psalm 146:1.

humble and devout thanksgiving, and grateful and loving meditation on the generosity and grace of God.

"How is a person able to achieve true purity and peace of heart?" you wonder. Hear the answer very briefly! Let them keep this verse from the psalm always in their mind, and commit it to memory, and recite it to themselves often: "Turn away from evil, and do good."[20]

The fulfilment of this injunction includes shielding your mind against wicked fantasies and negative thoughts, guarding your tongue against all malicious and harmful speech, and prohibiting your hands from all illicit acts. Behold, in doing this very simple thing, you will receive every blessing from the Lord and an abundance of mercy from the God of our salvation!

Resolve, therefore, O Reader, always to think upon what is good, to speak only what is good, and to do only what is good. Then you will attain perfect peace, and your conscience will enjoy untroubled serenity. For peace unfailingly comes to all those who are good, humble, merciful, straightforward, self-disciplined, and obedient to God, to the Church, and to their legitimate superiors.

But woe to those who are wicked, sinful, deceptive, perverse, proud, and disobedient! For they hurt no-one more than they hurt themselves, and they cause no-one more pain and distress than they inflict upon themselves.

---

[20] Psalm 36:37.

xii.
The Vice of Vainglory and Self-Satisfaction

"Do not extol yourself on high!" This is the lesson taught to us by the humility of Jesus. Do not glory in yourself—you who, without God, would be merely dust and ashes. Even when things go well and you are prosperous and successful, strive to be humble and restrained. For you do not know what tomorrow shall bring, and whether you will stand or fall.

In his letter to the Romans, St. Paul wrote: "Do not aspire for what is exalted, but be filled with fear and reverence."[21] Do not be proud in prosperity, lest you fall into evil. For God resists the proud, whether they are angels or humans. He draws away from all of those who presume upon their own merits or feel complacently and smugly pleased with themselves."

Alas, pride lurks as a veritable snare, ready to capture each and every single one of us in its universal dragnet—superiors

---

[21] Romans 11:20.

and subordinates, masters and servants, peoples of the world and religious alike! Pride is a highly contagious virus, ready to infect the heart. It does not spare even those who are chaste and devout, and those who are righteous and innocent, and those who are educated and powerful. On the contrary, it will often target such persons especially.

Who is there among mortals who can boast of being so chaste that impurity does not hide somewhere within the depths of their heart? Who is there among human beings who can claim to be so innocent that they do not ever experience any malicious thoughts in their mind? Truly, not one of us![22]

O God, You alone are holy; You alone are the Lord; You alone are the Most High, Jesus Christ! You were before all others, and You are blessed above all others, including angels and saints, and all things visible and invisible. Therefore, I pray to You, Lord God, heal my soul, for I have sinned against You. Create a clean heart within me and wash away all my sins, so that I may be completely pure and innocent, and completely Yours, and completely pleasing and acceptable to You.

And let me recognize my own failing and defect—let me be wretched and undeserving in my own eyes. For only then I shall find grace and mercy before You, my Lord Jesus Christ, and in the presence of all Your saints, both now and forever. Amen.

---

[22] Obviously, Jesus Christ and the Blessed Virgin Mary are understood to be exceptions to this generalization.

xiii.

The Various Contentions and Attacks of the Wicked, and the Necessity for Patient Endurance in the Face of These

Fight against those fighting me! For those who attack me are many.[23]

My Friend, since you wish to follow Christ devoutly and faithfully, much patience and endurance will indeed be necessary for you in this life; and most especially, you will need the grace of God strengthening and supporting you, in every place and at every time. For there are many, many wars and conflicts, both big and small, which are going on in this troubled word at all times. There is much labor and pain everywhere under Heaven. But in Heaven itself, there is none at all!

Who could possibly comprehend, describe or enumerate all the evils which take place in this world, and all the

---

[23] Psalm 34:1

misfortunes and calamities which befall the sons of Adam? And equally, who could ever explain the hidden judgements of God and their secret and unseen operations? Who could explain them except for God Himself, who alone is the supreme Judge, both strong and kindly, both just and merciful, both inescapable and patient? It is God who will ultimately conquer all the evils of mankind, and God who, in His mercy, sends the light of the sun and the rain from the clouds to sustain both good and evil alike.

There is no-one who can conceal themselves from the eyes of God and from His judgments, anymore than one can escape the sun and the radiance of its illumination. None can avoid His judgments, for God sees deep into the recesses of the human heart, and there is no-one who can evade His all-powerful hand, whether it descends in mercy or in punishment, to give or to take away. In every location and at every time, the all-perceiving eye of God is upon both the good and the evil.

Say to yourself, therefore, with the psalmist Kind David: "My eyes are always upon the Lord, for He has rescued my feet from the snare."[24] And, "unless the Lord helped me, my souls would have very quickly sunk into the pit!"[25]

O Reader, do not place your hopes or your aspiration for peace and happiness in mankind, nor in any created thing

---

[24] Psalm 24:15.
[25] Psalm 93:17.

either in Heaven or on earth. In you do so, you are certain, at some point, to be led astray, to be deceived, and to fall into confusion and disappointment. Salvation, and our perfect peace and happiness, comes from the living God alone, who is the highest good, and who alone is eternal. For it was God who created everything which exists out of nothing, and who rules and governs all things according to the mysteries of His often hidden but always perfect judgments.

xiv.
The Malice and Ill-Will of the Wicked against the Innocent

*O Lord, treat kindly those who are good
and right of heart!* [26]

Blessed are those who walk in innocence of heart in Your presence, O Lord, and seek You in honesty and true simplicity. Blessed are those who, in all their actions and words, and above and in all things strive for Your praise, Your glory, Your love, and above all Your will. Blessed are those who seek and claim nothing as their own, but esteem everything as belonging to God and attribute ever good thing they do or possess purely to His grace.

O Reader, may Jesus abide in your heart, in every place and at every time, in your work and in your rest! Let there be no dissimulation or insincerity about this, and do not crowd Him out by internal grumbling and self-pity. Rather, strive to behave as a good servant of God, and be ready to obey His behests and wishes at any time of the day or night.

---

[26] Psalm 124:4.

But it is not thus with the wicked! No, there is not fear of God before their eyes, nor love of God in their hearts. And, in the end, they will become like dust which is swept from the face of the earth by the wind.

What is it that rules and directs the thoughts and the actions of the wicked? It is certainly not the love of God; but rather it is the mouth which speaks unjust and deceitful words, it is contention and conflict; it is pride, envy, greed, fraud and depravity! Such indeed is the life of the godless and the wicked. And such people never cease to feel malice and ill-will towards those who do not share their own wickedness, and hence they constantly strive to disturb and corrupt all good and straightforward persons. But have no fear, for, with God's protection, they will not succeed!

For God has ordained everything in perfect and simple justice. Those who are good will receive good things from His hand; while those who are wicked will receive the just retribution for their wickedness. The good will receive the prize due to virtue, while the wicked will receive the wages of sins—namely, torment and eternal death.

O Lord, grant us the strength and wisdom to persevere in the ranks of the good, by cultivating the virtues which please You and make us into better people, and also by shunning the vices which separate us from You and Your goodness. In this way, may we rejoice forever with You in the company of the saints and angels. Amen.

xv.

The Envy of the Devil against the Salvation of Human Beings

*It was through the envy of the devil that death
first gained entrance into this world.*[27]

And it is from this original diabolic envy that all of the conflicts, contentions, disputes and feuds which have plagued the human race ever since have taken their origin. Woe to the devil, the Prince of Darkness, and the king over all the offspring of pride! Even today, he ceases not to test and disturb the faithful who strive to serve God.

In the beginning of his career, he sowed discord among the angels in Heaven, dividing them between those who served the Most High faithfully, and those who chose to join his own rebellious band. He was responsible for the first conflict between human beings and God, when, through disobedience, we lost the Garden of Paradise. He was also responsible for the very first disagreement between

---

[27] Wisdom 2:24.

Adam and his wife, Eve—though, alas, Eve prevailed in this, drawing us all into a whirlpool of sin!

It was the devil who sowed envy in the heart of Cain, and so led him to slay his brother Abel. And it was the same devil who gave rise to the estrangement and deceit between the brothers Jacob and Esau.

Today, the devil still wanders the earth, back and forth, attempting to pervert the instincts of humanity. He causes people in the world to mock those in religious life, and also (alas!) many of those in religious life to treat secular persons with scorn. He generates the mutual antipathy which so often exists between the learned and the unlearned, and between the clever and the simple.

Such mutual antipathy has become, thanks to the devil, characteristic of our human society, giving rise to misunderstandings, conflicts and the failure of charity. We see it between:

- the humble and the proud;
- the strong and the weak;
- the great and the small;
- the beautiful and the plain;
- the noble and those of common blood;
- the old and the young;

- those who love to travel, and those who prefer to stay in one place; and,
- those who are talkative, and those who are quiet.

Thus it is not only between the good and the evil, and the virtuous and the vicious, that the devil sows discord, but between all differing classes and types of people. For he is the source of all the disharmony in our hearts and in our society.

May the Lord Jesus Christ deign to guard and protect us against the devil's wiles! For by His cross, He has conquered the Prince of this World; and by His precious Blood, He has liberated us from Satan's tyrannical grasp. And He lives and reigns with the Faither and the Holy Spirit, God forever and ever. Amen.

xvi.
The Armor of Christ and the Saints against the Vices

O Reader, take up and put on the armor of God! Then you shall be able to resist in the day of evil, and to stand firm in the sight of all the world and all the Heavens. "Who perseveres until the end, that one will be saved."[28]

But if anyone falls or slips in any way, or they commit some offence, they should not immediately despair and give up hope. No! Let them quickly repent and cleanse themselves of their guilt by penance; and, in the future, let them guard themselves more carefully against such things and strive to amend themselves. How sound is this simple and encouraging advice! For it serves to fight against all evils of action and of speech. It promises to the one who resists evil and does penance for sin the reward for merit. It promises eternal joy and salvation for whoever successful corrects themselves, no matter how great a sinner they may have once been in the past.

---

[28] Matthew 24:13.

Hence it was that when St. John the Baptist was preaching the coming of the Kingdom of God and teaching detachment from worldly things, He said: "Repent and do penance; for the Kingdom of God is at hand!" And the Lord Himself said: "They *will pour* into your lap a *good measure*—pressed down, shaken together, and running over."[29]

What is this armor of Christ, you may ask? This is not a physical suit of armor, but a spiritual one, which is worn not externally, but on the inside. It consists of works of charity and humble service of others, prayers, tears of compunctions, and fasting and other acts of self-denial. And the weapons which the humble person who wears this armor must be the cross of Christ, the nails of His crucifixion, the lance which opened His side, His five sacred wounds, and memory of everything else which pertains to His holy passion.

The *gold* armor in the spiritual warfare is the most holy names of Jesus and of Mary, and the names of all the saints who are devoutly invoked as intercessors and protectors.

The *silver* armor is the words of Sacred Scripture, the writings of the doctors of the Church, the teachings and laws of the Magisterium of the Catholic Church, the rules of the various religious orders, and pious and devout prayers. Among these components of the silver armor of

---

[29] Luke 6:38.

the Christian should also be counted the moral examples of humility and obedience in the lives of the saints.

The shining *brass* armor of the spiritual warfare includes the battles of the holy martyrs and the torments which they so courageously sustained for their faith. For in these struggles and sacrifices they overthrew the vain idols of superstition and error, and exalted the name of the crucified Christ above all the kingdoms of this world, and above the very stars of Heaven! Let the memory of them and their heroism be a strong shield and support to you at all times, and especially when you face any difficulties, opposition and sorrow.

The strong *iron* amor of the spiritual warfare consists of penitential practices and actions which demand firm self-discipline—fasting, hard labor, long vigils, and acts of self-denial. This includes the shedding tears of compunction over sins, enduring heat during the summer and cold during the winter, burdensome work in the times of harvest, and patiently putting up with whatever pains of body or anxieties of mind you may experience from time to time. Such things will equip you with the discipline necessary to subject the vices of the flesh to the control of the mind, and thus to resist the temptations of the devil.

The weapons of faith which are particular suited to widows and matrons are chastity, modesty, quietness, humility, honesty, sobriety, and abstinence from luxuries and vain ornamentation of themselves. These should be accompanied by a willingness to be content with the household they manage and caution in going about in public. They should carefully cultivate firm custody of both the mouth from gossip and the eyes from curiosity.

O most, merciful Lord Jesus clothe us in all the forms of spiritual armor described above, and so defend us from the all the perils with which the devil, the ancient enemy of our souls, assails us. In this way, and helped by the intercession of all Your saints, may be merit to arrive safely securely to glorious Your presence, who live and reign forever and ever. Amen.

xvii.
The Usefulness of Frequent Prayer

"May prayer to the God of my life be with me,"[30] in every time and place.

O Reader, wherever you may be, may prayer be with as your constant companion and source of consolation. It does not matter whether the time available to you is short or long; it is always sufficient for prayer.

It is written in Sacred Scripture, and acclaimed joyfully every day in the holy Mass, that "Heaven and earth a filled with Your glory. Hosanna in the highest!" If you wish to pray effectively and powerfully, simply recite this short verse, and mediate upon its depths.

Offer to God your own heart, fully and completely and without reserve. Say to Him, "O Lord, You who dwell in the Heavens, I beseech You to save me, bless me, and sanctity me! Let Your divine will be enacted in me and through me at all times." And if you dispose your mind and

---

[30] Psalm 41:8,

intentions rightly, then everything you do and everything you think—every thought you have about God, or Sacred Scripture, or the mysteries of theology, or the virtues, or the human condition—all of these will become prayers and acts of supplication.

For all of these things, if done with sincerity, knock upon the door of Heaven and seek entrance into that blessed realm. All of these things amount to a humble imploring of the mercy of God. And whenever you do such things and think such thoughts for the glory of God, you may be assured that the holy angels in the celestial Kingdom rejoice, that demons are confounded, confused and frustrated, and that, in some mysterious way which may be totally imperceptible to you, you contribute also to the salvation of your brothers and sisters. For in your own prayerful disposition, you will also dispose everyone you encounter to prayer, even without saying a single word.

Therefore let your mouth cease not from prayer, your hands cease not from doing good works, and your heart cease not from holy meditation, nor your feet grow slack in responding to the call of divine service! When you arise from your bed at night, let prayer arise with you. Let prayer be your companion as you keep vigils and sing the psalms. Let it rest with you in your bedchamber. Let it go before you and follow you as you take you place in choir. Let prayer sit beside you in the refectory, and teach you in the classroom. Let prayer be your companion as you give thanks to God for the meal you have consumed. Let prayer be your companion as you wander through the fields, or care for the plants in the garden. Let it wash with you your feet, from all impure, wicked or imprudent words. Let it wash with you your hands, from the stain of sinful actions.

Yes, let prayer be your constant companion whether you are alone or with others! May it sit with you in silence, and be your helper at the beginning, in the middle, and at the end of your labors; to the glory and praise of the Most Holy Trinity. Amen.

xviii.
Short Private Prayers—Spears against the Enemy

*The Heavens stand firmly through the
Word of the Lord; and the Spirit of
His mouth is their strength.*[31]

The Word of God is a shield which protects and guards the faithful soul. It is also a sharp spear which is capable of repelling and destroying the enemy. Many and manifold are the frauds and deceptions of our ancient foe, the devil! And he never ceases to launch his attacks—which include temptations, vices, vanities, fears—against the devout and simple. But Christ, who is the wisdom and the strength of God, is more powerful than anything or anyone else in all the Heavens and all the earth. Yes, by one single word, Christ is able to conquer Satan, and to crush him to dust underneath His feet.

---

[31] Psalm 32>6.

Therefore, my Friend, have the Word of God, and select verses of Sacred Scripture, at hand for every occasion. If some sudden fear or anxiety rushes upon you, then read and pray: "Be to us, Lord, a tower of fortitude, in the face of my enemy."[32] If it is the urgings of the flesh which tempt you to some vile or contemptible sin, then read and pray: "Govern my flesh by fear of You, for I am in awe of Your judgments."[33]

If unjustified and wicked suspicion ever infects your mind, then read and pray: "Create in me, O God, a clean heart, and renew a right spirit within me."[34] If self-indulgent sadness or melancholy weighs you down, then read and pray: "Grant to me, Lord, the joy of Your salvation, and strengthen me with a good spirit."[35]

If vainglory or pride ever puffs you up, then read and pray: "Not to us, O Lord, not to us, but to Your name give the glory!"[36] If despair or desperation ever threaten to crush you, the read and pray: "O Lord, You have been my hope since my youth. Since I was in my mother's womb, You have been my protector."[37]

---

[32] Cf. Psalm 60:4.
[33] Psalm 118:120.
[34] Psalm 50:12.
[35] Psalm 50:14.
[36] Psalm 115:1.
[37] Psalm 71:5-6.

Whenever tedium or resentment with your life or with your wok begins to occupy your mind and dull your interest in things, then read and pray: "Help me, o Lord, and I shall be saved; and I will meditate always upon Your justice."[38] If you feel that sleepiness or fatigue is getting the better of you, then read and pray: "Illuminate my eyes, O Lord, lest I fall asleep in death, and lest my enemy says 'I have prevailed over him.'"[39] If boredom and sameness of routine start to extinguish your enthusiasm and make the fire in heart grow cold, then read and pray: "Lord, stir up Your power, and come to me! Strengthen me by Your word, lest I should fail on the way."[40]

If you feel that the demands of your work are excessive and that you are barely coping, then read and pray: "See my humility, O Lord, and my labor; and excuse all my failings."[41] If wrath or anger flares up within you, then read and pray: "Give patience and peace to You servant, O Lord, lest I lose the crown of glory. For You indeed have declared, 'In patience, you will possess your soul.'"[42]

If you recognize that ambitions for higher status or the desire for human praise and adulation start to creep into your heart, then read and pray: "Incline my heart, O God,

[38] Psalm 118:117.
[39] Psalm 12:4-5.
[40] Psalm 79:3.
[41] Psalm 24:8.
[42] Luke 21:9.

to Your testimony, and not to love of gain. Turn my eyes so that they will not gaze upon vanity; make me live in Your ways."[43]

If you are excessively tempted by fine foods, or to immoderate consumption of either food or drink, then read and pray: "The Kingdom of God is not food or drink, but righteousness and peace and joy in the Holy Spirit."[44] And, on the same occasions, call to mind: "It is the spirit which gives life; the flesh profits nothing."[45]

If you are filled with curiosity to hear about new things, or with a desire to look upon new sights and new people, then read and pray: "All the glory of the daughter of the king comes from within."[46] Reflect to yourself that all earthly things passing, and that all secular desires and possession are vain and ephemeral, no matter how beautiful they may be. In God alone is the fullness of goodness and lasting happiness to be found. If you follow Jesus and renounce your attachment to everything else, then you shall possess all things in Christ!

After all of these words of Sacred Scripture have been enumerated, there is one verse which you should retain in your mind above all else. It is this: "It is good for me to cling to God, and to place all my hopes in the Lord!"[47]

---

[43] Psalm 118:36-37.
[44] Romans 14:7.
[45] John 6:63.
[46] Psalm 44:14.
[47] Psalm 73:28.

xix.
Helpful Verses and Short Prayers for Use Throughout the Day

I have hidden your words in my heart, so that I may not sin against You.[48]

A human being will quickly slip into evil, unless he takes constant care to cultivate and nurture good things in his heart, as a constant reminder of the goodness of Jesus, our Saviour and God. So that you may always have God in mind, try to arrange your life so that almost everything that you hear and see, and all that that you read and think about, draws you to God in some way. Strive to be mindful of the name of your Lord and God all day and all night, so that everything will go well with you. For without such mindfulness of God, things are sure to go badly, no matter where you are or what you do. Such is our human nature and such is the world we live in!

---

[48] Psalm 118:11.

It is useful to have verses and short prayers at hand, which you can call to mind at the various occasions of the day and night. These will serve to promote this mindfulness of God, so that you will never stray far from Him.[49]

When you first awake for prayers, before the sun has risen, open your eyes, and read these verses and say to yourself: "Arise, O Sleeper, and Christ will shed His light upon you, for He has promised a crown to those keep vigil and prayer with Him!" When you hear the second signal summoning you to wakefulness, then immediately say to yourself: "Behold, Jesus Christ, the Spouse is coming! Those who arrive late at His presence will be disappointed and will miss out on a blessing!"

When it is time to commence your daily labors, then say to yourself: "In the name of Jesus Christ the Nazarene, arise and walk! Do the work enjoined upon you diligently, for obedience is more pleasing to God than any other sacrifice."

When you are engaged in your work, continue to pray often. Mediate on the verses of the psalms, avoid gossiping and idle chatter with your colleagues, and call upon the name of Jesus in your heart, inclining your head or even genuflecting as you do so.

---

[49] The description of the events of the day here are typical of monastic and religious life at the time, but many of them will also be applicable to persons in other states of life.

When you hear the bell sound, recite the 'Hail Mary,' and commend yourself devoutly to our blessed Mother's protection and care. When the signal is given to come to the prayer of the Divine Office, then say to yourself: "This is the sign of the great King! Let us go and offer Him our gifts, of gold, myrrh and frankincense." Whenever you enter into a chapel or church, say to yourself: "I shall enter into Your house, O Lord, and I will adore at Your holy temple, in reverence for You."[50]

When you stand assembled with the others in worship, to pray the Divine Office, say to yourself: "In the presence of Your angels I shall praise You; I will adore You in Your holy temple and proclaim Your name."[51] When you depart from there, let your thought be: "Lead me, O Lord, in the path of Your mandates; for these do I long."[52]

When you go into the sacristy, call to mind this verse: "Truly, this is a holy place, in which priests and ministers prepare themselves to celebrate the divine mysteries." When you climb the stairs to go to your dormitory, say to yourself: "I ascend to my Father and to your Father, to my God and to your God. Alleluia!"[53] And when you descend upon these same stairs, say: "Zacchaeus, come

---

[50] Psalm 5:8.
[51] Psalm 138:1-2.
[52] Psalm 118:35.
[53] John 20:27.

down quickly! For it is fitting that today I should remain in your house."[54]

When you enter into your private study, say to yourself: "Open to me the gates of justice; once I have entered through these, I shall proclaim the Lord! Here is my place of rest forever and ever; here will I dwell, for this I have chosen." When you are called to go out for some purpose, then call to mind the verse: "O Lord my God, direct my path in Your ways. Lord, I will follow You wherever You go, for You have the words of eternal life." And when you return to the privacy of your chamber, say with gratitude: "Lord, it is good for us to be here! Let us make three tents—one for Jesus, one for Mary, and one for the whole Heavenly host."

When you hear the signal begin given for lunch, then say to yourself: "Blessed are those who eat their bread in the Kingdom of God! My food is this: that I do the will of my Father who is in Heaven." Before your first taste of the food, call to mind the verse: "You will feed us with the bread of tears, and You will give to us tears in plenty as drink."[55] If the food or drink happens to taste bad or be of poor quality, then say to yourself: "For food they gave my gall, and in my thirst they offered me vinegar to drink."[56] Call to mind that when Jesus died upon the cross, He

---

[54] Luke 19:5.
[55] Psalm 79:6.
[56] Psalm 68:22.

was offered vinegar, and, having accepted it, He said to His Father: "It is consummated," and, inclining His head, He gave up His spirit. Blessed are those who share in the death of Jesus, for in this way they merit to arise with Him in glory!

If, on the other hand, the food and drink served to you is pleasing to your taste, then recite to yourself the verse: "How sweet to my throat is Your word. It is more delightful to my taste than honey from a honeycomb."[57] Yes, how sweet is Your Spirit, O Lord, and how great is the multitude of delights which You have hidden for those who fear You!

Before commencing any work, say to yourself devoutly: "Our help is in the name of the Lord, who made Heaven and earth.[58] Let all I do be for the praise of God." You should also pray thus at such times: "Be with me, God almighty—Trinity of Father, Son and Holy Spirit. Abide beside me, O merciful Virgin Mary, with Jesus your beloved Son and my Savior!" At the conclusion of your work, pray thus: "To God be thanks, to God be praise, for all the good things He has created!"

Before commencing reading or study, recite the prayer: "O eternal Wisdom, open my eyes, and I shall ponder the wonders of Your law. Send forth Your Spirit, and let

---

[57] Psalm 118:103.
[58] Psalm 123:8.

all the virtues and gifts of grace arise within me." At the end of your studies, place the book carefully back in its place, and recall what you have just read. In every word of sacred learning, and indeed in all knowledge and wisdom in every field, you shall discover something of the Bread from Heaven. But this is only if you understand wisely, and apply the knowledge you have acquired to living well. But if you do *not* use it for living well, or abuse your knowledge for wicked purposes, you shall not find therein any nourishing bread at all—but only a hard and indigestible stone!

Finally, on every occasion direct your heart to the humble and merciful Jesus. For in Him shall you find unfailing solace for your soul. Yes, every adversity and trial you encounter, will, through His grace, be converted into good and finds its consummation in the joy which endures forever.

The Seven Gems of Virtue

The generation of the righteous shall be blessed.[59]
But the ways of the wicked will perish.[60]

Truly, the gracious blessing of the Lord rests upon the heads of the just. But accursed indeed are all those who deviate from the commands of God!

In every individual or community there are seven distinctive gems of virtue which shine forth. When these seven gems of virtue are observable, there are sources of delight for God and His holy angels. But they fill demons and evil spirits with fear, loathing and disgust, and thus they repel their attacks.

The first of these gems of virtue is holy obedience. This brilliant gem is observable when there is perfect readiness to follow the instructions of legitimate superiors and authorities. In this way, each person is prepared to set aside

---

[59] Psalm 111:2.
[60] Psalm 1:6.

their own preferences and inclinations, emulating the obedience of Christ Himself, when He said: "Father, let not my will, but Yours, be done.[61] Yes, Father, let Your will be done,[62] for in it abides all goodness." By imitating this attitude of Christ, the virtue of holy obedience will grow and be made strong, while the wiles and machinations of the devil, who sows rebelliousness and self-will, shall be frustrated. Through holy obedience, the first of the seven gems of virtue, the joys of celestial glory are attained.

The second of the gems of virtue is agreement and concord within a community about their manner of life. The sign of healthy faith community is that they should not be disagreements and divisions about how work is to be done, or about practices in prayer, fasting, and devotion. This cultivation of harmony, peace and mutual support is in accordance with the counsel of the apostle St. James, who writes: "Support each other in prayer, and you shall be saved!"[63]

The third gem of virtue is stability, both of spirit and place. A person adorned with this jewel will not lightly change or abandon their situation in life and vocation, but be strongly committed to them. Such a person will not be constantly on the look-out for how they can advance themselves or make their life more comfortable or easier,

---

[61] Matthew 26:39.
[62] Matthew 6:10.
[63] James 5:16.

but rather they will be stable and firmly constant to their present commitments, regardless of the difficulties they may encounter from time to time. In this way, they express their unwavering loyalty to Christ, who has called them to the particular situation in life which they occupy. By cultivating this virtue of stability, they shall be among those who merit to hear from Christ: "You are those who remained with Me in all My trials."[64]

The fourth of the gems of virtue is patience in the face of adversity. This beautiful jewel of patience manifests itself in a readiness to endure what is hard or demanding in this present life, for the sake of the eternal life which is to follow. And this does not mean only being willing to sustain hardships for their own eternal salvation, but also to promote the salvation of others.

Wherever a group of people of diverse ages, backgrounds and dispositions are gathered together to form a community, it is very rare for conflicts of one kind or another not to arise. Such conflicts and differences are expressed both through words and actions, and are a part of our human reality. In such instances, which are virtually inevitable, it behoves us to put into practice the counsel of St. Paul: "Bear each other's burdens; for in doing this, you will fulfill the law of Christ."[65] Daily experience teaches us what these burdens are, and how they are to be borne.

---

[64] Luke 22:28.
[65] Galatians 6:2.

They include not only physical frailties and infirmities, but also the various weaknesses of soul and the deficiencies in virtue which are part of our human condition. And we all have these, for no-one is perfect except God alone!

The fifth gem of virtue is gentleness of speech in dealing with one's confreres, the nurturing of charity and kindness, trying to minimize outbursts of anger, and encouraging peace and mutual understanding. In a community in which this fifth gem of virtue shines forth, no-one will deliberately hurt or offend another—either by actions or signs, or by jokes or jibes, or by cruel words and insults. Rather, each person will love Christ, and be attentive to His teachings. For He said: "Learn from me, for I am meek and humble of heart; and you shall find rest for your souls in this world, and eternal life in Heaven."[66]

The sixth gem of virtue is sincere gratitude for the benefits conferred by God. It is expressed by praising and blessing God for all the good things He has bestowed upon creation since the beginning of the world, and all the good things which He shall continue to bestow until the very end of the world. Such are the blessings conferred by God that they fill Heaven and earth. So vast and awesome are they that no-one can explain them or count them. Therefore, all thanks should be given to God! It is indeed fitting that every creature should praise and thank Him; and

---

[66] Cf. Matthew 11:29.

however great this praise and thanks may be, it can never be sufficient for what He has done and continues to do.

The seventh and final of the gems of virtue is determined and faithful perseverance until the very end, in all of the other virtues described above, and the multitude of other virtues and works of charity and piety which flow from them. It is this virtue of holy perseverance which led the good and faithful servant of the Lord who received the five talents to accumulate five more. It was this virtue of perseverance which merited for him entrance into the joy of his Lord, into the celestial rest of eternal peace. And, if we cultivate it, it shall earn for us the very same reward, and admission into the same Heavenly homeland—where, with Jesus Christ and all the saints, we shall rejoice in glory forever and ever! Amen.

THE
WAY OF THE
MONK:
A HANDBOOK FOR
SPIRITUAL WARFARE

i.

The Straight Way to Reach the Kingdom of Heaven

The way of the righteous is a straight path, and the journey of the saints to Heaven is laid out for them clearly.

"What is this path?", you ask me. It is through endurance and hard work. For this is the way that will take you straight to the Kingdom of Heaven. "Is there no other way I can get there?", you enquire. No, my Friend, there is not!

"Is the *only* path to eternal life really the way of the Cross?", you ask me. Just so. Christ Himself taught this in His words, and by the example of His most holy life. In His words and examples, He taught us this way, and He calls us all to follow Him. And if you consider all of the saints, each one of them has followed this straight and royal path until the very end of their lives, to attain the magnificent prize of everlasting glory. They have all taken to heart and put into practice those words of the Lord: "Enter through the narrow gate, which leads unto life."[67]

---

[67] Matthew 7:13-14.

If you ask anyone who has chosen to follow the monastic life diligently: "What do you do in your cell?", he will reply to you: "I pray, and I read, and I write. For in doing this I gather spiritual honey to strengthen and refresh my soul." Very well and wisely has he answered! For those who have chosen the monastic way should burn with constant zeal for the ongoing improvement of their souls.

If you ask the person committed to the monastic way: "What do you do when you attend the Liturgy of the Hours with the community?", he will say to you: "I read, I sing, I praise the Lord! And I mourn in penitence for the sins of the world." He has responded to your question correctly. For the Liturgy of the Hours ought to praise God, in the jubilation of the psalms, and to repent for sin in their lamentation. In this way, the good monk is united with the choirs of angels in Heaven, who do preceisly the same thing.

If you ask the person who was embrace this monastic way of life: "What do meditate upon in your spare moments, such as when you are occupied with eating?", he will tell you: "I am mindful always of the sacred wounds of Christ! I consider every single wound He bore, as much as I am able, and I mourn deeply for each and every one!" Very wisely has he answered!

If the soul is more important than the body (as, indeed, it is), it is fitting to meditate upon the life of Christ and the words of Sacred Scriptures while nourishing the body with food. For meditation upon the life and passion of Christ nourish and heal the soul, even as physical food sustained the body[68]

---

[68] This reflects the monastic custom of reading from Scripture and other spiritual writings during meals.

ii.
Custody of the Heart and the Mouth

I said, 'I shall be watchful of my ways, so that I may not err with my tongue'.[69]

Take care never to be idle or overly talkative. Do not be overly curious about other people's business, and never be a mocker or indulge in jokes at other people's expense.

When you are engaged in your work, remain mindful always of the Lord your God; and guard your actions and words carefully. In this life, wherever we may be, we are always surrounded by enemies or potential enemies. Indeed, we make the voyage of this mortal life over stormy, perilous and treacherous waters!

Therefore, my Friend, you should pray without ceasing, or the temptations and trials which are always at hand will soon get the better of you and you will find yourself

---

[69] Psalm 39:1.

sinking into the dark depths of sin and despair. Stand strong, and do not slacken for a moment in your efforts in the daily battle of life.

There are, my Friend, three particular treacherous and savage beasts of temptation and vice. Beware of these three beasts! These three beasts of temptation normally appear at particular times of the day. In the morning, it *sloth* that you must guard yourself against, for it will prevent you from entering fully into the gift of the day that God has given you. In the middle of the day, it is often *gluttony* which strikes, when the urge to seek gratification or stimulation through excessive consumption appears. Finally, in the evening, it is often the *lust* of the flesh that attacks the heart.

These three vices are like three beasts. Sloth is like a dog, for like that animal it longs to sleep away the long hours of the day. Gluttony is like a ravenous wolf, whose appetites can never be satiated no matter how much it consumes. And lust is like a rutting donkey, a beast which knows no rest from the urge to sow its proverbial seed wherever it may.

Consider for a moment how each of these animals is best tamed and controlled. For a dog, you need a stick. This stick is the fear of death, for it is a sure antidote to the temptation to waste the precious gift of life in sloth. For a wolf, you take a sturdy and heavy staff. This heavy staff is the fear of the fires of hell, for it will certainly make you think twice before indulging in gluttony. Finally, to tame and control a stubborn and wilful donkey, you need a whip. The whip which will tame the donkey of lust is mindfulness of the passion of Christ and the torments of the martyrs.

If you arm yourself with these three trusty spiritual implements, then you will surely conquer the daily attacks of each of these three vices—the dog of sloth, the wolf of gluttony, and the donkey of lust—with no difficulty at all, and emerge free and victorious.

iii.

Frequent Invocation of the Names of Jesus and Mary

Help me, O Lord, and then I shall be saved![70]

Endeavor to call upon God in all your work—in the morning, at midday, and at evening. If you do this, you will certainly be assisted powerfully by Him in every need of your body and soul. Have the holy name of Jesus always in your heart, and you will be clean from all stain of sin and all impurity. Keep the beautiful name of Mary constantly upon your lips, and you will be filled with all the consolations of the Holy Spirit.

The weapons of the one who would follow the way of the monk are solitude and silence, and prayer and fasting. Work hard in the day, and pray and keep vigil at night. These activities are the special secret weapons of all the saints.

---

[70] Psalm 118:117.

By doing this, you will please God and His holy angels, and frustrate all the demons who would lead you astray. To the young and to beginners, these things are hard and demanding, but very useful. To those who are old and experienced in the ways of the spiritual warfare, they eventually become delightful and natural. To the lazy and indolent, they are always irksome and hard; but to the devout they are found to easy and pleasing.

If you ever find yourself unable to keep vigils at night when you wish to do so, be content with calling upon the holy name of Jesus. For this will repel all attacks of the enemy.

If, for some reason or another, you are unable to sleep at night, then invoke the holy name of Mary, and salute her with joy. For if you do this, the angel of the Lord will be with you, as your friend and companion, and will accompany you through the long hours of the night.

If you ever find yourself unable to concentrate on prayer or unable to motivate yourself to pray, then simply meditate on the psalms as best as you can. And the Holy Spirit will come to you to comfort you. This Holy Spirit, who is always with those meditate on Scripture, will be to you the very best of teachers, and the greatest illuminator of your heart!

iv.
The Daily Battle Against Vices

The Kingdom of Heaven is taken by force; and the forceful are obtaining it.[71]

My Friend, equip yourself with the invincible weapon of the holy cross, and fight like a strong soldier! Work and study as if you were a good and diligent scholastic; prayer as if you were a devout and holy monk; work hard like a faithful and tireless servant of God. If you do all of these things, then you are guaranteed to receive a glorious crown in the Kingdom of Heaven!

The best way of removing one nail is with another nail. The best way of conquering vice is by cultivating virtue. The virtue of silence, if judiciously applied, suffocates and kills the vice of wrath. Fasting tames and extinguished the vice of gluttony and over-indulgence. Sloth is put to flight by disciplined hard work. Flippancy and irreverent joking are overcome by cultivating gravity

---

[71] Matthew 11:12.

and compunction. Fraternal charity and compassion help to cure the noxious virus of hatred. Your enemies can often be turned into your friends simply by treating them with kindness and courtesy.

The cultivation of patience will gain for you the precious prize of peace of heart. On the other hand, those who are quick to point out the faults of others will win for themselves only hostility and resentment from their peers. By involving yourself in as few matters of business as you possibly can, the more peace will experience. Conversely, if you involve yourself in many matters, then your inner peace will inevitably be reduced.

"The less business you do, the more peace you will have. The more business you do, the less peace you will know." This is an axion which you should often repeat to yourself, and often call to mind. It is very simple to express in words; but, if put into practice, with the help of Christ and for His sake, there is no principle which is more effective in acquiring serenity for yourself. If you know this and put it into practice, you will certainly have peace!

There are many people in this world who talk too much; but very few who prefer to keep quiet. There are many people eager to acquire an unlimited number of possessions; but few who are content with just what they need. In truth, human beings are made in such a way that we are never fully content, unless we enjoy the very highest good, which is nothing other God Himself!

∗   ∗   ∗

Just as a dinner where there is no bread served and no salt available must be regarded as defective, so it is that a meal without sacred reading is lacking something essential.[72] A meal without reading does not provide satisfactory nourishment, for instead of the Word of God, one generally gets inane small talk. The best dish to serve the soul is the hearing the Word of the Lord, and deep rumination upon its hidden meanings. Whoever takes their refreshment in sacred reading is nourished by the most delightful of all foods. But the person who prefers to listen to empty vanities and trivialities will find themselves empty, malnourished and parched, for the fare they are consuming lacks real substance.

---

[72] In monasteries and religious communities, meals are usually accompanied by sacred reading, and eaten in silence.

V.
The Greatest Things for the Soul

I will love you, Lord, my strength.[73]

Among all noble human qualities, there is nothing more noble than virtue. Among contemptible and despicable human qualities, there is nothing more contemptible and despicable than vice. Among qualities which are beautiful, there is nothing more beautiful than chastity. In the field of learning and the pursuit of knowledge, there is nothing more profound than contemplative wisdom. Among the holy writings, there is nothing more sacred and profitable to the soul than the Gospels, for they tell us about the life, death and Resurrection of Jesus Christ, our Savior.

Among all prayers and acts of praise of God, there is nothing more holy and effective than the Lord's Prayer, taught by Christ Himself. And there is nothing sweeter and more pleasing to the holy angels than the 'Hail Mary.' The Lord's Prayer surpasses all the other prayers written

---

[73] Psalm 17:1.

by saints through the ages. For it contains within its few lines all the oracles of the prophets and all the mellifluous richness of the psalms. It expresses everything which it is necessary for us to pray for. It praises God in the highest manner, and unites our own soul to God. It raises up our earthly concerns to Heaven, and penetrates the very clouds of the firmament, and flies above the choirs of angels to rise up to the very throne of God Himself.

Blessed indeed is the one who meditates deeply on every single word spoken by Christ!

vi.

The True Inner Consolation
of the Soul

To the one who conquers, I shall give the
hidden manna. I will give him a white stone on
which is written a new name, which none
shall know but himself.[74]

This 'hidden manna' promised here is the consolation of
the Holy Spirit, arising from the sure hope of mercy and
sincere contrition for sins. This consolation of the Holy
Spirit is what imparts to people good intentions and the
firm resolve to amend themselves and to make progress in
their spiritual journey.

God is truthful, and all His words are true and firmly
established and reliable. A faithful and true friend does
not lie, nor does he deceive or mislead. But whoever does
deceive or mislead another does not have the truth in him.

---

[74] Revelation 2:17.

Whoever becomes puffed up with pride because of their possessions or achievements becomes displeasing to God. Strive not to be proud of what you have—for the very greatest thing you have, which is the promise of eternal glory in Heaven, you were given freely, not because you merited it or earned it in any way.

Take care not to create scandal around yourself by sin, vice or impiety; on the other hand, do not actively try to build up a good reputation for yourself. And do not assume (as many do) that you are somehow more holy, more devout or wiser than others.

A good name and good reputation are the natural consequences of leading a good life and practicing honesty and humility. Whoever conducts themselves poorly will very soon undermine their name and their standing. But the person who repents and turns away from wicked or dissipated ways will, in due course, acquire a new and better name for themselves.

Yes, the person who sincerely repents and resolves to amend their life is like an infant that has been newly born! From the moment they resolve to walk in the Spirit and to cast aside all that is harmful, they begin to live a new and better life.

The good reputation which is the natural outcome of true sanctity of life adorns a person more wonderfully than the fragrance of precious ointments and the splendors of limitless wealth. Strive for goodness of life and character, and a good reputation will naturally follow it.

vii.
Calmness of Heart through Silence of the Tongue

My secret is my own.[75]

Whenever you find yourself involved in long conversations with others, you will find yourself distracted and a multitude of thoughts, ideas and feelings will be stirred up within you. When this happens, return to yourself and work to restore your tranquility, by silence and solitude. Weep for any sins or faults you may have committed in your words or deeds.

When the memory of things you have seen or heard distracts your heart, apply at once the remedy of internal prayer. In this way, you will expel all harmful images from your mind and cast away any superfluous and burdensome cares which may plague you.

---

[75] Isaiah 24:16.

The person who longs for nothing at all on this earth will find themselves freed from all argument and tumults, for there is nothing here which he is seeking to gain or win, or to prove to others. The soul of a person who is genuinely free of the bondage of worldly desire will be able to ascend, in their heart, to the peace of Christ in Heaven at any place and at any time. Thus spoke St. Monica, the holy mother of St. Augustine, when she said to her son: "Come, let us fly, filled with faith, to the Heavens!"

viii.
Effective Remedies for Vainglory

Every man living is vanity! [76]

Do no extol yourself before others, nor seek to be extolled by others, for any good thing you have done or any good quality you possess. For God know very well that you have many internal faults and failings which these other do not see. Indeed, many of these internal faults and failings which you have, even you yourself do not see—or, if you do recognize them, you do not fully comprehend just how grave and serious they are.

The person who seeks out human praise for themselves often falls into anxiety and confusion. Very often, people who seek out praise end up earning disgrace or embarrassment for themselves instead! For others people easily detect their motives, and come to see them as ridiculous.

---

[76] Psalm 38:6.

Vainglory and love of human acclamation and praise has deceived many. For it directs the heart away from the desire of that which is truly good, and which endures forever. What could be more foolish than to seek the vain, ephemeral and empty glory of this passing world, at the expense of eternal and true glory? What could be more deluded than to care about what other people think, and to neglect what God Himself thinks? What could be more insane than to desire the things of this earth, which are all insufficient, passing and deceptive, and to treat with disdain the promised treasures of Heaven?

The heart of those who love riches is tied to the earth—this fleeting realm of sorrow and trial. But the heart of those who are truly detached, who are truly poor in spirit—such a heart is bound to nothing but Heaven!

The heart of the humble person places itself in loving obedience to God; but the heart of the proud raises itself up against Him.

ix.
Purifying the Heart from Vices and Hidden Passions

Blessed are the pure of heart.[77]

Purify your heart from all vices, so that you may become truly good and innocent. Why do you wish to be praised for merits which you do not really possess? Surely you recognize that you have many faults—as, indeed, we all do. If all of your secret vices and wicked thoughts and passions were revealed to others, would you not have much to blush about, and much to be ashamed of? But if anyone else ventures to point out one of your faults or failing or to identify one of your vices, you will be indignant and offended; when you should, in fact, be thanking them for doing you a service.

Who are those who love what is empty and foolish? Those who love human praise.

---

[77] Matthew 5:8.

It is the person who is humble and aware of their own shortcomings who stands solidly in the truth. Such a person does not raise themselves up upon delusions, but remains firmly grounded. Such a person recognizes themselves as a sinner always in need of God's grace.

My Friend, examine yourself carefully. Look deep into your own heart and at what lies hidden there. Do not be quick to give credence to any bad things or gossip you hear about others. The faults of others are not your business; it is your own faults you should be concerned about.

Very often have I seen the kind of people who praise their friends to their faces; but, behind their back, will criticize them and speak ill of them. On the other hand, I have seen observed another type of person—those who will honestly criticize and correct their friends to their faces; but then earnestly defend and excuse them before others.

In people of this second type, charity and truth have met and act together in harmony. Where such is the case, peace and well-being will follow.

My Friend, wash your hands clean of the pollution of all perverse deeds, and restrain your lips from idle and thoughtless words. Turn your eyes away from sights which harm your soul, and protect your heart from the contagion of wicked thoughts and desires. If you do all of these things, you will be clean and pure in the presence of God.

Reflect on the fact that you regularly wash your face and your hands, so that you will be acceptable in the presence of other human beings and not cause offence. How much more does it behoove you to wash your conscience, so that you will be acceptable before God and His holy angels, who see into the innermost depths of the human heart!

x.

The True Peace of Heart which Results from the Virtues

Blessed are the peacemakers.[78]

God loves the heart which is pure and clean. Christ abides in the heart which is at peace. The Holy Spirit rests upon the heart which is humble and meek.

But, O Reader, if you become immersed in tumult and distraction, you will lose the sight of Jesus. In mockery and flippancy, you will offend Him. In anger and wrath, you will cast Him out from your presence. In lying and practicing deceit, you spit upon Him. In gossiping and speaking hurtfully of others, you despoil Him of His garments. In hating your brother or sister, you are crucifying Him!

Indeed, whatever hurtful actions or sins you commit against your neighbor, you do to Christ Himself. For He

---

[78] Matthew 5:9.

declared this quite clearly when He said: "Whatever you do the least of these, that you do unto Me."[79] Take care not to offend God; and take care not to offend the image of God, present in each of your fellow human beings.

Call back to the right path those who are have gone astray; and instruct, with all humility, those who are ignorant of the truth. Strive to give an example, in your actions and in your life, of all that is good and holy. Follow Jesus devoutly by patiently enduring offences and insults. In return for the evil and wickedness which other people do against you, offer only righteousness, charity, and justice.

And do not forget that for the small and passing tribulations which you suffer in this present life, you will receive an eternal prize—namely, everlasting joy with the saints and the holy angels in Kingdom of Heaven! Amen.

---

[79] Matthew 25:40.